Bad Man Radar

By Esperanza Moreno

Table of Contents

Introduction

How many times as women, do we find ourself blind to love? We fall in love so fast, yet miss very important signs. Signs might be the thing that saves our lives. In general we shouldn't focus our lives on negative energy. This energy will not feed our growth. When we pick a partner. We want those qualities to build us up, as well as our man. It can be very easy to fall into hatred and pain. By watching for certain signs, we can avoid much of the heartache. We can take a step back and find someone who helps us grow. This book in no way is a perfect illustration. Although, being a woman I have found these signs very helpful. And it feels amazing to help others avoid psychological damage or to keep them from developing trauma.

Manipulation

The moment you try to leave your man they attempt suicide or say they will. You have a fear that they will go through with it. Although, they only do this in order to reel you in every-time. Overtime this becomes their tactic at making sure you don't leave. Many times this will occur with weaker personality traits. Another tactic used is manipulation. When you are in his grasp, is when he has the most control and say so. As your relationship progresses he will say that, "If you love me, you I'll do this." This statement is only a lie to draw you back into his vicious cycle. Love is not measured based on how much you do or whether you do something you don't wish to do. This tactic works best because of our emotional senses. We take this to heart and this really kills our insides. Although, no need to be frightened. You still love him even if you don't have sex right off the back. A man that respects you will wait and not force upon you his own expectations. These types of men know just how to get to you. They know what makes you sad and they know what will draw you back in. For instance, some men before they break up will say things like, "you never loved me anyways." These are key statements that linger in our senses and make us feel weak. These personal attacks are what bad men use to dig at out hearts.

Doubt Casting

Dating can bring many challenges. One challenge is the self hatred that fake love brings. When bad men get ahold of you, they work hard to control your mind. They want you to believe no one will like you. They want you to believe that you won't find someone better. This is a well known myth men do to manipulate you into being dependent on them. Men know very well what you are capable and you can get any man you want.

Men also will guilt trip you into believing that someone will be better than you. They try to say how bad of a girlfriend you or wife. They spit verbally on everything you have done for them. Also, men will make you feel no one will want you. They say how miserable they are with you and how much pain you are to have. I must confirm that all of these are lies to draw you away from having the person you really need. True love is not abusive love.

Flowers For His Sin

One great theme in the lives of love, is fake love. Identifying this type of love is crucial to saving yourself from heartache. Throughout the time of dating your guy, you will notice they seem to bribe you. For instance, one day you and him are fighting. You make up. He buys you flowers and the day ends. As time goes on you start to see this pattern. Fights always end in a way that doesn't seem finished. Yet the guy will keep gifting you things. These gifts are the perfect tactic. Why? Because he is using this as a tool against you. Every-time you get into a fight. He will mention, "don't you remember all the things I have done for you." More than likely these "things" are the stuff he bought you and not the actual actions he has done. This is a great tactic for men because it makes us feel guilty. We feel that we should feel sympathetic and feel bad that he did all this for us. However, in all actuality he did do those things, but worse things followed. Even though he was: taking you out to dinner, giving you money and giving you excessive things, he didn't have his full heart in this. Surely, as you stay with him longer. You will notice the amount of things he does for you decreases. He starts making you feel you don't deserve them. He will go out of his way to stop these things completely. A bitter deception lies in this. We can't hold onto him solely because of the things he has done, especially when has done worse too much. We become blinded by these gifts and these self talks. We become blinded by his sweet words and sweet charm. All of these are great sins we take in. We believe them to be happiness. This happiness is fake and temporary. We can only function on real happiness. This means that, the guy genuinely means what he says and his actions don't conflict with that. So if he says that "he doesn't want you hurt" and he goes and abuses you, this is wrong. He is going against the very foundation he built with you. You are trusting him based on his words, but his actions are causing you severe damage. This damage isn't just something "you get over." This damage will affect: your future children, you health, you happiness and those around you. We cannot ignore the mere consequences of these actions. We believe that somehow this person is right for us. We won't find anyone better right? Our mind is our greatest enemy. Men know this. We have to take out the greatest weapon, our mind. We have

to see that he is only using gifts and
bribery to attack us.

Blaming You, Without Blaming Themself

A relationship indeed will never be perfect. Not everyone will make the right choices and not everyone is fine tuned. We must not forget that there are limits to fighting. Fights shouldn't be happening every week and they shouldn't progress into traumatic events. During fights there is a certain thing that bad men do. Whenever you fight with them, they are going to end that fight blaming you. They want to make sure that you are the only reason. They don't want to hear what they did wrong. They want to hear what you did wrong.

You really need to pay attention to fights. Does he blame you right away? Is he willing to hear your side? Does he seem to run away when it gets difficult? Does he avoid solving issues all together? The key here is to look at these signs and don't let him continue to toy with your mind. If it's been four fights in and he still blames you, don't stay. Staying I will say, makes matters much worse. When we stay, we show him we are dependent on him and that he has control over us. WE got to be STRONG. Don't let his words break you, let your heart take you.

Forced To Have Sex

From the start of a relationship, there needs to be boundaries. Sex is a boundary that shouldn't be crossed by force. If you aren't ready for sex, your man may force you to be. He will claim, "sex is love and you dont love me if we dont have sex." Sex is more than a temporary act, it as an act that bonds two people. A guy who wants to have sex when he just met you isn't one that wants commitment. Most guys who have sex too early and by force want to leave you. They have one objective in mind and once they get that they leave. This isn't made up or fiction. I believe we think that, "this couldn't happen to me." It really can happen. This is why being aware is important. No matter what age you are watching for these signs is helpful. As soon as a bad guy has sex with you, he will become distant. He will stop showering you with gifts. He will stop romancing you. He only wanted sex and thats what you were for. As things progress they lack empathy and dont care about what you want. During the stage of sex they will practice it badly. They wont wear protection and they come on to you when you say no. You tell him you are waiting till marriage and he still rubs himself on you. He isn't having respect for your choices. You need a man that respects your goals and doesn't lure you to fall off track. Dont take risks with a man who is willing to risk it all barely knowing you. No matter if you have sex or not you still love him. Dont let him make you believe sex is the only way to love someone. During sex if you already have had it, does he only concern himself with his own pleasure? Does he only have sex purely to pleasure himself? This is a selfish act and you dont deserve sex that gives back. If you always find yourself not pleasured and very sad this isn't a good sign.

Bad men will also become obsessed with sex. No matter what if your ready or not they want sex. They force you into sex everyday and only want sex their way. Even if your uncomfortable, they dont care. They start to say, "trust me I know what im doing." They dont keep you safe and take too many risks. They physically force you into sex. All of these signs are not good at all and usually are a sign of being used. Sex becomes so obsessive that they wont let you leave without it. Some signs to look for is: he says how sexy you look, he bugs you about sex a-lot and after saying no he keeps forcing sex. If your man believes it is ok to force himself onto you, he isn't the right guy. Love is an act that should be made with mutual sex. Sex should never be non mutual.

Romanticism

Many bad men start out with a lure. Romance is a key to manipulators. he first date will start out with flowers. They will take you to a nice meal. He takes you on the romance streak of a lifetime. He seems so charming and so sweet. How could this be better? Wrong, its just getting started. He is making himself so appealing that you will suddenly give into sex and whatever he needs. He will buy you everything you want. He will spoil you and make you feel special, then suddenly he has sex and things change. His true colors come out through sex. You will notice after sex: he will go out less, he doesn't baby you and he doesn't give you affection. He will put less effort into the relationship and fall back into his true self. They are more dull and they start taking back gifts they gave you. These are signs they are not interested in a long term relationship. Dont be fooled. Find someone who puts in his effort your whole life, not just for a month.

Not Supportive of Life Goals

Some issues that arise in a relationship with your man is that he wants you to live like him. He suggests to you hows you should handle your life and how to live your life. These qualities are a sign that they want to have control over your life. Don't let this sign go unnoticed. Another sign is when he takes you away from your family. No man should consume you to point you abandon your family or feel trapped with them in the holidays. This consuming behavior will alter your lifestyle and make you less involved with people outside your home. As a result, depression can stem from this. Some men will even suggest the idea to uplift your life and move suddenly. This idea is a bad idea if you only know your man for a short time. Many men will use this to keep you where they want you, not where your family needs you. Without your family, it makes it easier for a man to control your daily life. Any suggestions a man says like, living a car is not good. Ideas that are not sustainable and not grounded don't last. A good man will be stable in his life and want stability for the chance of having a family.

Another issue that arises is a man saying, "you are lazy and don't do anything." I must tell you this is a great lie. Bad men use this to degrade women and to keep them suppressed. A manipulator needs your consent to have your control. Thoughts are what men use to get deep inside our emotions. If a man says, "you need to grow up." In reality, all these insults are what your man is. By attacking you they try to cover up their scheme. Comparing is also another issue with bad men. If a man starts to compare you to him, know that this comparison is unrealistic. No one should be comparing you to themselves or expecting you to do what they can't. There is limits in relationships don't let him cross them. In this phase he will tell you, "you would be worthless without me." Let's be real, you have a lot of worth without this guy. He just doesn't want to admit that he has nothing to offer. He will shower with doubt and make your life miserable. Everything you do will not be good enough and no matter what you say he's not convinced. If it is safe, don't be scared to challenge his doubts with the truth. You have more than him, this is his fear. You are actually a very capable woman and this his worst nightmare. He will insult your living situation and your life. Be sure not to let him convince you that you haven't seen rough patches before. We all go through pain and sorrow. Don't let him make you believe he is the only one. The biggest picture here knows that your man insults you to hide his wrongdoings.

At times your man may become hypocritical. You start to notice that everything he does isn't punished, yet you are. Men will shield their sins, while you are beat with yours. Remember that if he can do it, why should you be blamed? How can you be at fault for something makes look ok in his own actions? Let us be honest, he is jealous of who you are. He sees how accomplished you are. He doesn't want you to grow beyond him. His ego screams for you to be below him. Don't be his footstool.

He Lives With His Parents

During the younger stages of dating a man there are simple problems. If you notice a 24-year-old man living with his mother and father this should ring bells. This should be heightened if his parents have issues with him staying there. If a young man has issues with his parents this is not a good sign. A bad relationship with his mother or father can rot the very foundation of your relationship and if he isn't willing to get therapy, you know the solution. A mother is supposed to show their child what a man should be. Don't forget to see your man's relationship with his mom. These moments are key to reading his standards in life.

Judgmental of Your Situation

~ They say you aren't doing enough

~They insult your progress and

capabilities

~They tell you to take on more tasks

~You ask them to change. Change

doesn't come. They make up excuses.

~They say you have too many

expectations

~They feel they aren't wrong you

are.

~Every time they say they will stop

they don't.

Alcoholism

When it comes to a bad man's habits, drinking is one. If your man is drinking a lot. If they can't control how much they drink this can cause issues. There is even greater risk when they are emotional or aggressive while drinking beer. Having no self control is an obvious sign of no self control of their actions.
Every-time he picks up a beer, you find yourself embarrassed. You start apologizing for your mans I'll behavior. Just remember, he chose this behavior not you. We can use excuses for so long before they break. Another issue is when he insults you while drinking. He gets up in front of your family or at home. He starts to insult you in every way and afterward act like it didn't happen. This cycle

shouldn't be an every Friday type deal. If your man consistently doesn't try to do better, when will they? Drinking is bad when it turns into physical and verbal outbursts. Don't let your man take the lead in these situations. You must remember he should be embarrassed, not you. This is a good indicator of how a man controls his life. If a man has moderation, he is more likely to have respect. The final red flag in this situation is rejection. If your man refuses to go to therapy for their addiction, this is unhealthy. Everyone knows if you don't get help you will drown in it. Don't let them have the power to drown you. If they refuse it, don't be apart of their life until they fix it. There is no use waiting for a man to change, when they have well overstayed their visit.

Threats

As the relationship progresses you find that your man no longer has limits. He starts to say threats. For example, "if you leave, you will have nowhere to go." The threats start out small. As time moves on the threats get bigger. There is then a progression of threatening physical harm to you. As this becomes the case, this is not good. Outside help is needed at that point and even before. Threats can even turn into a show of physical strength, such as: throwing objects, grabbing arms or breaking objects. These behaviors are a result of heated anger. Anger then leads the man to act on impulse. Threats should be taken seriously, as situations can escalate depending on the guy. The relationship over time becomes an if, then pattern. As soon as you get sucked into this, it becomes toxic. A relationship shouldn't be a show of power and control.

Verbal Abuse

Emotional Attacks

Ex) "You are overly emotional"
"You never listen to me"
"You never know what I want"
"You are a bitch"
" You never do anything
around here"
"You are a psychopath"

-Threats- they threaten to kill you or
threaten you to do things or you will
be humiliated.

Physical Abuse

All of us women in our lives have been through something. Many of us have been raped, beaten and verbally abused. One idea that toxic men use is the idea that women don't have life as bad as them. Realistically, women do indeed have many traumatic and horrible incidents that shouldn't be squashed. What a toxic guy will do is, he will hurt you and make an excuse for it. "Oh I'm sorry, I'm just really upset right now. You don't know what it's like to have an abusive mother." In this moment us women feel compassionate. We think, "oh poor guy." In reality, he just hurt us and didn't take responsibility for it. I believe that in my own life I have been through many traumatic incidents as a woman. I in no way say mine is greater than anyone's.

Although, I try my best to not use my trauma as an excuse to bully someone. In reality, men are just as capable as women at controlling their anger. We shouldn't feel bad if our man constantly uses this excuse over and over again to justify his sick actions. What men are doing when they use trauma to harm you, is they are becoming the abuser. Instead of developing an understanding that abuse is wrong and shouldn't be repeated, they continue the cycle. Some signs to look for in a toxic relationship include: physical hitting, use of force sexually and physically and they have no respect for your boundaries. Another idea to watch out for is "physical harm." When a man puts his hands on you, he is more than likely going to do it again. Sadly, staying with an abusive partner can make the physical harm turn into death. Many women have

the idea, "that won't happen to me."
We believe somehow the situation
will deplete. We think that someone
capable of beating is to the pulp, isn't
capable of killing us. Now, I think
that can't be ignorant to this idea.
Don't be the woman that lost her life,
over a man. I believe women have
too much value to bow down at
abusive men's feet. I believe many
women are scared of the idea of
reporting incidents or women get
scared that people will judge them.
Hiding behind your home with an
abuser is no different than walking on
the street with a person you don't
know after dark. Both are not safe
and you already know the ending.
Getting away from this environment
is something that is very important.

Obvious Sign List

-They physically hit you.

-They force themselves onto you.

-You tell them you're not ready for

sex and they still want it anyways.

-They ask for nudes and sexual

pictures or videos within a short time

of being together.

-They have no respect for your

decision on sex.

Emotional Absence

If you ever find that during the course of your relationship that your man doesn't have emotional empathy, this can be disastrous. A lack of emotion makes it easy for an abuser to inflict harm without remorse. This also makes the abuser able to deny you of the security you need with your own feelings. Without feeling reassurance, it can be a downfall. We can only push so far until we collapse. If we go through an emotional time, we need someone to relate to our understanding of pain. They don't have to go through what you have, but they need to have an understanding of how human suffering feels.

Health Declines

One sign that typically gets ignored by us women is health. When in a toxic relationship, we begin to decline. Our body becomes ill and we lack the self-care we need and we suddenly are depressed. Our outside life seems dull and interactions with people seem meaningless. Our body is so weak it becomes fatigued and has a lack of motivation. We become very sick and start to believe we don't deserve to be well. We start to eat ourselves emotionally and become less focused. Days begin to drift and we feel life has no meaning and no worth. If our man says we are worthless, we must be. Wrong. We must take hold of our health and gain back clarity. We must rid of this toxic relationship and begin to start self-

care. Once he has your health, he
has your life. Don't let him take it.

Conflict Never Resolves

Fighting in relationships is a very
evident
quality of a toxic relationship. One red flag is when your man constantly fights with you. When conflict is always occurring, this is not a good sign. If conflict is healthy it will be resolved and it wont arise everyday of the week. Something that will happen in this situation is that your man will act like the conflict resolved. The next day will come and your man will keep fighting. He wont do anything to fix or change things. If he does fix things, its only temporary.

As a result, fighting will lead to a break up. When you are fighting it turns into a cuss battle. He wants to express himself but he wont listen to you. He blames you for the issue and doesn't admit his mistakes. In this stage he will possibly leave and not want to solve the conflict. He will walk away and not want to find a solution. By not finding a solution, it sets the relationship up for failure. This creates more conflict and less understanding. Eventually this explodes into a violent break up, which is not safe or healthy.

No Protection

A foundational structure of a relationship, needs a basis of protection. Your man should be ready to protect you from harm and have remorse for the harm they have done to you. He shouldn't be saying, "it's your fault this happened to you" or "get over it." Knowing the nature of suffering, these words are the start of emotional wounds. You have to remember that you deserve to be protected. Your man also shouldn't say, "it's your fault they hurt you." These are personal attacks at you and are emotional manipulation maneuvers. These are used to make you believe that you are the reason, you are sad. There is no accountability for your mans actions or any unmoral actions he lets happen by others. What I mean by this is, when people are against you he takes their side. He will let others hurt you and not blame the person for their actions. He will act like you had it coming. For instance, "you wore that dress. It is your fault he touched you." These are lies that bad men use to feed your mind. Don't believe this because you are not always the reason. If you were innocent, your man shouldn't be stirring the pot.

Another big issue is he wont check in on you. A day goes by and you say nothing. He goes about his day and doesn't check in with you. A good man will check in with you and make sure you are ok. Many issues arise when your man can spend his whole day not worrying about you. Your safety should always be on his mind and be a concern. He emotionally should want you safe. If he doesn't care about you being safe, dont waste your time.

Cheating

In many relationships cheating is a big deal. Cheating is considered as something that is a deal breaker in many relationships. I have to say in my experience, cheating isn't a joke. If your man says, "it's not a big deal," this is wrong. Your man should take cheating seriously and not sugar coat it. If he says, "it was an accident," this is a lie. In life we choose to do as we wish. We make choices and choose to make those choices. Don't let him convince you that he couldn't control his hands. In this moment he will act dumb. He will say that didn't do it and you find out through others what the truth is. If he doesn't admit the truth, he will always lie. At this point he has no remorse and doesn't have sympathy for the damage he has done. This leads him to keep you

and to keep cheating. Don't let a guy
use you in this way. He is abusing the
love you have provided and
constantly hurting your feelings. The
first time a man cheats is obvious.
The second time, is really pushing it.
I believe you are too valuable to
suffer through this "fake love" to
keep an an "abusive love."

Only Notices Your Flaws

A common theme in toxic men is noticing your flaws. A bad man wants to cause conflict and point out how bad you are. They say, "you dont appreciate me." This is a personal attack to get you to feel bad. Even though we both know its not true. You could give him the world and he says,"your lazy." At this point your man isn't appreciating what you do and making you look worse than you are. Don't let that take you. If your man is able to lie about you, he is able to harm you. This is a constant battle that shouldn't be fought to the death. Find a man that knows what your worth, not one who constantly wants you to change yourself.

Attacking What They Can't Understand

-You are in pain, and they don't care.

-You are emotional and they don't do anything.

-You are crying and they don't help you.

-They can see you cry and have no remorse.

-They don't ask and try to understand why you feel how you do.

-They start insulting you and don't have any idea how your feeling.

That's Too Much Work

Men who are no good will also act like simple tasks are burdensome. They claim that doing simple things for you is too much work. Even if something helps you they don't try it, but the moment you don't help them they will get mad. When your man doesn't want to help you, they refuse to make things better. They look at you as a project instead of a human being. Instead of saying they want to make you happy, they say making you happy is too much work. A man who loves you will not look at you as a burden and will want to do nice things for you. Dont feel you deserve less than you do.

Public Humiliation

One interesting phase is that an abusive man will put you through is humiliation. He purposefully makes you look bad in front of your family and anyone else. He makes clear that you are crazy. He insults you verbally. In this process, your man tries to make everyone believe that you are the issue and the downfall of the relationship. He wants others to believe that he is much better than you. He does this publicly or in your home. This involves verbal insults and usually involve others. He will make sure someone is present during an argument to make a fool of you.

Mistakes That Lead To Holding Onto A Bad Guy

-Believing they will change.

-A kid should fix this?

-I don't want to be lonely. Fear of being alone, leads to dependence.

-Dependence on the abuser (codependent women need someone to help them).

-Fear of leaving (the abuser will threaten them or won't let them leave).

-Attempts at suicide (using suicide to

bring a woman back in).

-Ignoring signs of ill behavior

-Self-denial- not believing that what

happened actually did happen.

-Manipulation- the manipulator draws

you back in with mean words and

emotional insults that dig at you to

make you come back.

-They say they love you, yet their

actions speak otherwise.

-You believe you will never find

someone else. Although, someone

better is waiting around the corner.

-Low self-esteem- an abusive
boyfriend lowered your self worth, so
you feel you are not good enough for
anyone. You feel you should stay
with them because you feel
unworthy.

-You give them a pass for physical
and mental abuse. (You blame
yourself and say it's your fault they
are bad).

Game Plan

Being a relationship can cause endless frustration and finding advice is a battle in itself. We must come to our senses and evaluate the situation. The first step that we should follow, is to make time away from that person. If we become distant to that person it breaks the emotional barrier. As women we tend to act based on our emotions. This can become an issue because we won't be able to fully examine what's happening. When we distance ourselves, the emotions we have become more stable. We are able to use our logic more efficiently. The biggest challenge with leaving someone is knowing what's best. Emotionally at the time it becomes difficult. Maybe you have a child with them. Maybe you are emotionally alone or in a situation that brings dependence to this person. Although, this man really knows that you are capable of being alone. He will squash every hope you have, only so you will believe you are helpless. I must tell you this is not true. This is the great lie and demise they use to take away a healthy opportunity. Sometimes one of the second steps is to examine behavior. When a guy is exhibiting any of a majority of these qualities listed in the book, this should raise a red flag. Emotionally you will be inclined to forgive the person, but don't let forgiveness be taken advantage of. If a guy is constantly breaking the rules, this means something is not right. Breaking up is one of the hardest events in our lives. We believe in the moment that nobody will be like this man. Personally I believe that women are strongest when they protect their own needs. This creates the third step. When you realize what he is doing. You must realize that he is taking away your needs. In order to be healthy and successful women, we need our needs met. When those needs aren't met we become distant and depressed. As woman we cannot be ashamed for our situation. The fourth step is knowing that you are not to blame for his sins. He can embarrass you all he wants. Although, he only does this to corner you into a wall. Don't let them have this must power and control. You are not any less capable. You are not any less beautiful. You are not alone. You are not worthless. You are not powerless. As you will soon see. He is trying to take out the very strength that you have. He knows how powerful you are. He knows how brilliant and successful you are. Don't let him take this. Step five is test him.

When you notice what he says. Does he consistently keep his word? Does he change his views? Is he still following the same cycle? Is he falling back into old patterns? By asking these questions, certain habits will arise. If you notice that these patterns keep occurring, it's best to say don't stay. As women we must understand that we are not the only people in charge of change. Men must change to. If your man has not changed. The results and your sadness will not change. This is no different than an addiction. The more we practice an addiction, the more we never leave it. We have to practice our strengths. This leads to the sixth step. We need to confront him on his doing. If the situation is more extreme, I would not suggest this. Although, in a safe situation I would suggest confronting them on their lies. Do they blame you for it?

Do they act sympathetic towards you? Do they get annoyed with you? Do they not say sorry? If they don't seem to react positively to your reactions, this means they are ignorant to change. In a relationship we will not grow without change. Change is the step we make since birth to become a better person. After seeing all of these signs step seven arises. Not only do we need to realize what they are doing wrong to us. We need to see what damage they have already done. Are you struggling with depression? Are you avoiding family? Are your daily tasks seeming meaningless? Are you more agitated than normal? Do you find yourself crying more than normal? Are you having thoughts of suicide? These questions are very important in the break up process. We aren't "breaking up" in all actuality. We are breaking away from a toxic situation.

If your health is at stake this is a serious issue. We should not deny the importance. If this occurs, I highly suggest therapy and to break up with that guy. The eighth step I will recommend is changing activity. As we break up with a toxic person, we still bear the sadness. This process does take time but don't feel rushed. Sadness only lasts so long before happiness comes. New activity can include: going outside, trying something new, doing things you miss doing and making more time with people. When we are in a state of loneliness it helps a lot to be around people and to be doing things we love. In the end, we need to love ourselves and remember all the qualities that a man should be loving that are in us. Don't wait until things get worse, to take action.

Dear Future,

I have talked about many of the
ways a man should not treat you.
Many of these ideas may scare you or
may break your heart. I surely know
they did to mine. The pain although
was worth the reward. It was worth it
to me to get out of such a toxic state.
A state that transformed my being.
When you are healed you will be
searching again for someone. I would
like to tell you some hints that will
help you. The first hint is, find a guy
that respects your opinion. When we
go through life and battle with issues,
we need to be heard. We need
someone to understand and be
patient with us. The second hint is,
find someone who protects you. You
need a man to protect you and get
you away from harm. If a man is
harming you, he is not loving you. I
believe that we need someone who
can hold us and tell us things will be
ok. In a healthy relationship, you

need a man that is your rock. You can't have a man that breaks you down emotionally and still be happy. The two do not go hand in hand. The third hint is, have a guy that brings you joy. A man should do what is practical to make you happy. He shouldn't spend his time finding ways to upset you. He should value your happiness and this should be his motivation. Everything he does needs to be a reflection of his love for you. As we know love cannot be harmful. A man should never overstep your boundaries. A final point I would like to make is, don't ever believe that you won't find someone better. Life tends to make us believe the worst when the best is yet to come.

Words Unspoken

"[B]ut just from what I've seen, women need to stop doing so much for these men that won't do half of the same shit the women are doing. Stop staying with him after he has: cheated on you many times, yelled at you, called you names, laid hands on you, and value yourself more than you are valuing these men" ~Andi Cucchiara

"Don't deny what you are capable of and what he is. He is just jealous. He is jealous you are what he could never be"~Esperanza Moreno